THE
MODERNITY OF SAINT AUGUSTINE

THE MODERNITY
OF
SAINT AUGUSTINE

by

JEAN GUITTON

Translated by A. V. LITTLEDALE

HELICON PRESS
Baltimore   Maryland

NIHIL OBSTAT: Hubertus Richards, S.T.L., L.S.S.
IMPRIMATUR: E. Morrogh Bernard,
          Vic. Gen.
Westmonasterii, die 14a Aprilis, 1959

The Modernity of Saint Augustine was first published in French, under the title *Actualité de Saint Augustin*, by Editions Grasset.

Made and printed in Great Britain by The Ditchling Press, for the publisher, Helicon Press, Inc., 5305 East Drive, Baltimore, 27, Maryland, in June 1959

66485

CONTENTS

To
my friends in Geneva

PREFACE

ST AUGUSTINE is one of my masters in the interior life. He was the chief influence in the formative years of my youth. For more than seven years, he was the subject of my daily meditations for a thesis I was preparing on his thought. I took care not to let my attention become fixed on a particular section of his work or on any one phase of his life (not even the antipelagian phase, the last, and highly important, one), but to keep the whole constantly in view, comparing himself with himself.

In studying a thinker who has had such enduring influence in the course of history, it is quite amazing to follow the variations in standpoint from which he has been regarded. If we had had to consider St Augustine in the seventeenth century, and to summarise the essence of his thought, our subject would inevitably have been that of grace. Now, however, we are mainly concerned with other questions: existence and creation in time, the stages of the spiritual life, history viewed in its totality, the definition of the Church, the relation between the history of the Church and that of mankind, the relation of Christ with the temporal order. At any rate, these were the matters that engaged me when, thirty years ago, I started on the study of St Augustine. It is difficult to conceive how these studies would be looked on by an Augustine returned to the present world, having discarded the accoutrements of his own epoch, and oblivious of the events of his personal history, the stimulus of controversy, the inevitable exaggerations of his expressions;—an Augustine, in fact, who strove to see his essential self, as he sees himself now in eternity. Would he, I wonder, look upon himself as a Christian philosopher of the school of Plato, or as the Doctor of Grace, or, as I try to see him, as the thinker who long in advance of all others gained some understanding of the nature of time in its relation to the life of the soul and of mankind in general?

Whatever answer, conjectural in any case, may be given to this question, my choice is made. My aim is to gain some idea of the kind of solution given by St Augustine to the various types of problem thinkers have set themselves on the subject of temporal existence. I agree with Sainte-Beuve that our ideas run along a few specified lines, that the problems confronting the human mind and the solutions proposed to them are not so very numerous. That being so, it seems to me that it is feasible to draw up a chart of these problems and of their possible solutions, and that this 'enumeration' will assist us in our choice. I have preferred to deal with those problems that here and now occupy Western thinkers, be they religious or not.

These problems are not by any means new, but they have been restated in forcible fashion: and, making use of St Augustine as a master, not dead but living and present, I have conjectured what he would have said and thought in the present time, this second end of the world. He had his wily opponents, Donatus, Manes, Pelagius; his somewhat doubtful allies, Plato and Plotinus; his friends, highly esteemed indeed, but so different from himself, Ambrose, Jerome, Paulinus of Nola; and I have looked for their replicas in our own time. I have always looked on doctrines as the roles in a drama, and on writers of past ages as the actors performing and transfiguring these eternal roles, each in accord with his vocation and his particular nature. Yet despite their originality, these actors cannot hide the fact that the text remains always the same.

It is on this account that St Augustine has helped me to gain a clearer insight into this harassed world, from the year 1924, when I first became acquainted with him, to 1954, when I wrote this small work. Through all these thirty years I have remained convinced that St Augustine's thought provides a commanding position from which to judge my own time, and is becoming constantly more relevant.

I could see the relevance of his thought after the upheavals of the first war, and at the time when the first stirrings of the œcumenical movement directed men's thoughts to the Church, when my own master at the Sorbonne, Léon Brunschvicg, taught the doctrine of salvation by pure reason in the universe of Spinoza and Fichte. It appeared more clearly still as 1938 approached, when we could foresee and dread a new 'fall of Rome' and an interval of barbarism in Europe. And anyone who reads these pages can see how the problems of existence, destiny, civilisation, the Church and hope that confront us in 1955, seem to me already present to the mind of St Augustine.

Consequently, when, on the occasion of the sixteenth centenary of his birth, those engaged in organising meetings of commemoration asked me to speak of his *actualité*, his relevance at the

present time, at Paris and, more especially, at
Geneva before the faculty of Protestant theology,
I agreed to do so. This work contains my
thoughts on the subject.*

11 *February* 1955

---

* This book was first published two months before the
new edition of my thesis, *Existence et Destinée, le temps et
l'éternité chez Plotin et saint Augustin* (Aubier), with a
new preface, which forms the final chapter of this present
edition.

INTRODUCTION

TODAY it is sixteen centuries since St Augustine was born, the 13th of November, 354. *Quindecim annos*, wrote Tacitus, *grande humani aevi spatium*: a long period in a human life. In the life of the human race, sixteen centuries is also a long period; but in that period there has been a constant revival of St Augustine. A Roman legend has it that three fountains sprang up from the ground where St Paul's head touched it three times. Likewise, we may say that St Augustine's thought touched Western history three times, and, on each occasion there sprang up a new stream: first, in the Middle Ages, when he became the inspiration of political and scholastic thought; then in the sixteenth and seventeenth centuries, when the Reformers and innovators drew from him their sustenance; and lastly, in modern times—the time of Kierkegaard and Hegel, Bergson and Blondel, Mauriac and Claudel—wherein his presence, though veiled, is yet so palpable. Perhaps, we might even say that the workings of time have brought to light his real depths; that the medieval Augustinism, which mainly brought out his latent Platonism, fell short of the Augustinism of the controversies on grace; that, though these disputes were seen to be inspired by him, it was reserved to the present epoch to share his most profound intuition, his conception of existence in time. However this may be, Newman was right when he said that St Augustine gave, as it were, 'a new edition of Christianity', and that he, 'though no infallible teacher, formed the mind of Christian Europe'. We are to look on him, as on St Paul before him, as a chance appearance of extreme improbability, coming just at the moment when the tree of Christianity in order to develop needed a new graft, redirecting, heightening, colouring, perhaps even altering with the addition of its dark substance the Catholic sap. Take away Augustine from the patristic age, Paul from the early Church, and the course of Western history would have been quite different.

When we commemorate the day of someone's death, we look at things from a human standpoint; we recall what he did in his short passage through history. But if we concern ourselves with his date of birth we adopt a divine standpoint; we set ourselves, unawares, the question of predestination; why, before this person came to be, had the author of all history chosen him out, what mission did he give him, just a fragile being newly come to this earth?

This is the question I hope to answer in some way at the end of this work in the course of which I shall constantly note St Augustine's modernity and the similarity between his time and our own.

I

THE INTERIOR MAN IN HISTORY

WHEN he was forty-three, twelve years after his conversion and Baptism, St Augustine wrote the twelve books of his *Confessions*, to give an account of himself, before God, to man: *Apud te, haec narro, generi meo, generi humano.* Of all his works none spread more widely. This incommunicable experience of his was of value for all; ten centuries later, minds so different as those of Petrarch and St Teresa of Avila were to find in it the story of their own spiritual course. Modern man, too, comes more and more to recognise himself in it.

So powerful was the Greek tradition, which ignored the historical factor in human knowledge, that this work, which echoed so strongly down the ages, remained neglected by philosophers. Psychology of the Aristotelian type studies the soul as one thing among others, and is concerned with detecting its way of functioning. The soul is made to reflect external reality as a mirror does. For this reason, classical psychology excels in analysing those two contrasting states in which the soul coincides with nature and is absorbed in it,

namely *sensation* and *intellection*. All that inter-
mediate activity in which the intellect gradually
develops and the will comes to life has significance
only in its relation to the pure activities of sense-
perception, understanding and decision. Now,
what we first discern in ourselves are individual
recollections, personal happenings, and it is
through these that man advances in self-knowledge. History is the very stuff of human consciousness.

It is then understandable that the idea of the
inner history of an individual never suggested
itself to the Greek mind. This was not because the
Greek, as is so often said, had no conception of the
'person', but rather because in the pure Greek
view there was no real connection between the
event and the person. The occurrences of life
were but the accidents, even the defects, of life.
Hence, for Aristotle, the magnanimous man is as
devoid of memory as of zeal. He does not speak of
himself any more than of anyone else. He is
exempt from passion, and is likewise without
history. It is the same with the wise man of the
Stoics, who neither remembers nor sins. If he is
converted to wisdom, it is a radical transformation
which fixes him immutably in that stage. He does
not advance, he is borne away beyond time. If his

life comes to be written we will be given a portrait of this superlative state. This is what Diogenes Laertius does for Pythagoras, Damascius for Proclus, Porphyry for Plotinus, Philostratus for Apollonius of Thyana. Marcus Aurelius, the mild emperor, does not describe himself nor write his confessions; but, in the context of events whose details he does not trouble to furnish, he compares himself to an ideal of impassivity, which he laments that he has not reached. When one of the ancient philosophers contemplates existence, he leaves out of account the most striking features of the human condition; and, if all the same he knows himself, he does so not by viewing the whole course of his life and drawing on a full memory, but by intuition of his essence, by recollection of those fleeting instants when he realised his type in the light of a moment of perfection and 'as he is at the end when changed by eternity'.

We moderns however, avid readers of novels and autobiographies, have become familiar with the idea that man lives in time, that he travels in a direction which cannot be reversed, that every moment of time has its value, its special savour, its eternal significance. This was not the case with the ancients, nor is it with the Indian philosophers; and Nietzsche himself, in his ecstasy of Sils-Maria, believed himself to have grasped the law of the eternal cycle: 'Let everything return in ceaseless repetition—this is the ultimate rejoining of a world of becoming with a world of being, the highest point of meditation'.

Why is it, though, that the idea of personal and interior history has been so little entertained by the mind of man? No doubt because, for most men, such a history is so uneventful. And perhaps, on the other hand, because in such a history something irrevocable has happened, and they want to blot it out altogether. This something we call *sin*.

The tendency of the Greeks was to look on sin as something that happened inevitably, like mischances in the world of nature; for them, the 'faulty' was never far removed from the 'fatal'. If we accepted the view implied by the great tragedians, we would have to reduce moral error to an aberration wrought by destiny, equate evil with insolence, and ascribe punishment to the operation of a natural and necessary law. Plato invariably looked on the wicked as sick men, and regarded sin as error. Certainly, Aristotle did not follow him in this confusion, for he specified the share of the will in human action; but with Plotinus we see revived, in a form scarcely different, and with a few elements taken over from Stoicism, the old popular notion that sin is a blot not affecting the inner being of the soul. It is held to be, as it were, the addition to the soul of an element which irks and sullies it, and which it ought to get rid of. The perverse man is abnormal, a monster. Sin is a kind of consent wrung from the soul by those evil passions that spring from its embodiments; rather than error, it would seem to be accident. Whatever the case may be, the wise man never sins, and could not. So, then, there is a mysterious link between the sense of (personal) evil and the sense of (historical) time: at every period when the sense of evil is alive, the sense of time is seen to be present. When the sense of evil grows weak, the sense of historical time, of the irreversible course of time marked out by particular events lessens correspondingly.

The history of the Jewish people provides an example of this profound relationship; for it is not too much to say that it was in Israel that the mind of man discovered the nature of evil. In this history we see man becoming conscious of history through sin, repentance, vocation and return. This happened at first in a collective fashion, the individual feeling himself guilty or called merely in so far as he was a part of the whole people; but the work of the prophets individualised this communal feeling. Ultimatèly there came a time when certain privileged souls among the Jews became convinced that in their own particular lives, obscure though these were, they re-enacted the whole history of the people. The duration of the whole was condensed into that of an individual, as in a mirror reflecting it. Each individual sinned on his own account, and each was converted. Each one was called by name. The mystery of Abraham was reproduced in each individual conscience.

Yet before St Augustine the history of personal sin, which is now the theme of modern tragedy, the gradual invasion of the self by the flesh usurping in us the role of the spirit and attempting to justify itself, the adjustment effected between the various parts of the self, the coincidence of the moment of liberation with that of the most strenuous resistance, the fluctuations of the deepest self which refuses, at the last, to identify itself with the flesh, and which, at the very time when it effects its detachment from the depths of evil, feels itself caught up in the depths of the good—this history had, as yet, found no literary expression. We may say that St Augustine is the first man in the West to have attained, in personal fashion, the experience the Jewish people had reached, in a collective way.[1]

There would, however, be little point in history if it consisted of nothing more than an account of what happened, or even of an explanation of events by their antecedents. History of that sort is only a section of real history, just as a map gives only an indication of distance and height. Integral history would be both *linear*, like human history, and *vertical*, like history as seen by God in his eternity, as made by him out of the material of our own history. It would be one in which the working of secondary causes would be seen related to that of the first cause. Nor are we to hold it to be impossible, for it is such a history that, using artistic symbols, the Jewish prophets (Isaias for instance) attempted to write.

St Augustine may be said to have tried to apply the rules of this kind of prophetical writing to his own personal history; he *tried to watch his own history unfold itself within the eternity which knows no change*.

What St Augustine calls predestination is precisely that vertical activity by which the moments of our historical duration are harmoniously adjusted one to another. In the *Confessions* he brings out, in the midst of the incidents and chance happenings of his life, the persuasive, insinuating, insistent, even secret, action which enlightens without dazzling, which draws out without compelling. It is an action which is the outcome of art, but of a divine art which disposes the will while leaving freedom intact. It can do so because the Eternal is more present to a being than that being is to itself; He is able gently to mould the heart. He can, too, make use of the most ordinary contingencies to endow the words and acts of our associates, without their knowledge, with a spiritual significance exclusive to ourselves. Sometimes by secret stirrings,[2] sometimes by the prompting of circumstances, God recalls the soul to itself. In the most unexpected ways[3] he makes it aware of its wretchedness,[4] consoles it and makes it run in his paths.[5] His hand is ever present to re-create and restore what he has made.[6] Furthermore, he knows how to make use of the evil that man does, for he does not cease to bring into order what he condemns: though he does not create it, yet he orders it to the good; the bitterness which permeates illicit pleasure is foreordained by his mercy, and the soul's consciousness of its disorder is itself a part of order, being the effect of a law.[7]

There is in consequence always a harmony

between the interior state of the soul and the
unlooked-for helps it finds, whether these come
from within or from outside itself. The most
perfect type of this harmony—which is at one and
the same time the end to which all the others
tend and the outcome they jointly prepare—is the
death of the righteous man; for his death is but
the coincidence of the end of his life with the state
of grace. Final perseverance, therefore, is nothing
else than the fulfilment of predestination.[8]

From this vantage point we may say that *time
can get the better of evil*; for the evil we have given
up is no longer evil. The actual occurrence
remains: it is written in God himself, whose
omnipotence cannot efface it, and cannot, for
instance, bring it about that Judas did not
commit his act of treason. But the act underlying
the occurrence changes its significance with the
repentance and becomes matter for homage, in
which consists 'confession'. *Duration* and *liberty*
are thus related. The substance of time lies
beyond the present; it is the final moment by
which the whole sequence is judged. The very
core of time is its tension towards eternity.

The account of the *Confessions* seems to give the
impression of a fore-ordained destiny. If God hears
our prayers, it is because he has already formed

them.[9] He governs us in a hidden fashion even in
our disorders.[10] Even a man's self-persuasion is his
doing.[11] Like other thinkers in their analysis of
freedom St Augustine restricted the sphere of free
will. But freedom is no more destroyed through
being upheld by a power of another order than is
time absorbed by eternity. These are two aspects
of one and the same problem. St Augustine
believed that our being overflows beyond itself:
there is more in our action than our own part in
it, more in the event than what we are aware of,
more even in freedom than the independence we
feel, more in prayer than the temporal petition.[12]

Consciousness gives out at the point where God's
action begins. When we pursue immanence to its
ultimate reach, we come upon transcendence.
When we have fully analysed the free act, we
discover the place where freedom is grounded.
When we penetrate the depths of time, we come
to savour eternity.[13]

That is why St Augustine could speak in the
same breath in terms of human freedom and in
terms of predestination, that is, of divine freedom.
If he was ever tempted to abandon the first,
he would be recalled to it by the memory of his
sins. If he forgot the second, he had only to reflect
on the gift of God, to be reminded of it. No one

was more convinced than he of the primacy of grace, and yet no one has ever described with greater precision the vacillations of freedom, the hesitancy of the will in its decisions. No one believes more fully in the transcendence of God and of his justice (to some his conception of God seems fearsome); yet no one has striven so much to grasp God's immanence, so respectful of human freedom.

The reality of succession is due to him who created time, for how could times succeed one another, unless he contained them all?[14] It is he, too, who gives value to history, for the events of history would be without significance, if God, by consenting to will himself in them, did not bring us thereby to will ourselves in him.[15]

*　　*　　*

Here, by way of parenthesis, I will pass over the intervening ages, and attempt a comparison of St Augustine's intuition with that of some modern writers, apparently at the furthest remove from him.

FREUD

The most remarkable case is that of Freud, for while he certainly seems to have felt no direct influence of St Augustine, to have had no acquaintance with his writings, Freud seems to have derived from Augustine at times his own opinions, at times his terminology. The *libido* is there in the *Confessions*, as also the idea of the pervertibility, the actual perversion, of infancy. Let us look beyond the differences: the modern techniques, the powerful, and often fruitful, myth of scientific precision and of determinism; and compare their general outlook.

We find both in St Augustine and in Freud the idea that the psychic life goes deeper than the conscious level; that our conscious arises out of a special sphere, the unconscious (which St Augustine calls *memoria*, the 'memory'); that the child is already a responsible person, although he does not know it; that his most natural acts, such as those directed to the breast which feeds him, are not pure but already tainted with perversity (which St Augustine, using St John's expression, calls 'concupiscence'). There the similarities cease, for St Augustine had not the least conception of the idea of *neurosis*; at any rate, those suffering from neuroses and mental disorders he looked on as among the 'possessed', about whom he drew his information from Scripture, paying due regard to individual cases when he came across them. The idea of finding a place for them

THE INTERIOR MAN IN HISTORY

in the natural order and considering them as sick persons could find no place in his mind; still less could that of healing these diseases by any sort of method other than that of St Mark's Gospel, fasting and prayer.

We may, however, conjecture what an Augustinian Freud or a Freudian Augustine would have been like.

Freud's whole system assumes that the spiritual world (not only the order of grace, but that of the mind in its highest activities) has no real, independent existence of its own—as if, consequently, all causality, all life, could be explained by biological factors, whether simple or complex: instinct and combinations of instincts.

No doubt, the idea could also be found in St Augustine that combinations of instincts bound up in the original warping of our nature from the time of Adam, have a sovereign power, since 'concupiscence' in the child is active in its pure impurity. He was, too, alive to the fact that self-knowledge could counter the force of concupiscence since his *Confessions*, taken as a whole, were an exercise in self-awareness written in order to purify and free himself. Finally, in St Augustine as in St Paul before him, can be discerned the idea that the defences erected by society, instead of assisting the struggle against *libido*, are liable rather to intensify concupiscence by exasperating it. From this point of view, we may see in St Augustine the first germs of the idea of 'repression'.

The difference is that, for St Augustine, the life of the unconscious from which emerges the ego is not a life of dubious value in which instinct, brought too soon to the level of thought, too soon conscious even in the unconscious, becomes perverted. Although his thought on original sin includes the idea of a sin committed unconsciously in Adam before the existence of the individual, it is yet true that this sin is but an accident of history, bound up with the *racial* fact of our belonging to the line of Adam. In the depths of his being, man remains bound to God; the source of our psychic life is above, not beneath, us. *Memoria* is at the same time memory of God and memory of ourselves.

Compare Freud on this question; indeed the comparison arises naturally since, as I have said, he himself made use of the Augustinian word *libido* to designate the carnal instinct become conscious. For both thinkers the tiny infant is already possessed by evil powers; the defences erected by society and rejected by him increase his feeling of resentment. But from his perception that the origins of our destiny are to be traced ultimately to the twilight of pre-infancy, Freud derives a materialistic theory of existence which tends to explain the higher elements of our nature—love, art, religion—as metamorphoses, sublimations, of the lower, making the spirit, in fact, but a hypocritical cloak for the flesh.

Suppose, now, we try to imagine what an Augustinian Freud or a psycho-analytical St Augustine would have been. All that is of value, all the wisdom and the healing qualities in the method of psycho-analysis would remain intact; yet what a change in significance it would undergo. No longer would the absolute from below (the flesh become consciousness) be called upon to explain the higher absolute, but it would be the likeness of the soul to God which would make itself felt, and which would be projected by becoming degraded, even into our carnal states and our unconsciousness. We would have a psycho-analysis in reverse. And so the idea that man is twofold, and not simple, as Freud's optimism supposed in spite of what is so obviously apparent, would explain our dissociations and interior divisions, not only by social inhibitions, but by the cleavage in man himself, caught between the temptations of the flesh and the call of love. Instead of the bio-social being set up by Marxism following Freud, we would have one which is both bio-social *and* spiritual, a 'mind-body' giving its allegiance to *value*.

It is not too much to say that a depth psychology of this kind, taking due account of the different levels of the psychic life, giving to the body what pertains to it, to the spirit its proper place, and to a higher light its rightful scope, has as yet never been put forward. We ought, too, to add that its time has not yet come, for the explanation in purely material terms (whether of the Freudian or Marxist type) must certainly be tried out first. Only the failure of this kind of 'explanation' will open the way to *spirit*. In all probability, modern man has to take this round-about way; he will not apprehend the spiritual directly, but only through the impossibility of an explanation which excludes it.

PROUST

A similar comparison could be made between St Augustine and some modern novelists.

What after all is the modern novel in so many cases but a remembrance indefinitely prolonged and orchestrated? No one, perhaps, has brought this kind of writing to such perfection as Proust. No one at any rate has held so strongly to the idea that, in recalling to memory time seemingly vanished we have, according to the mysterious expression of St Paul, a method of 'redeeming the time', of regaining a kind of eternity. From this point of view, Proust may be compared with St Augustine, and moreover it may be estimated how much this thought would have gained, had he been an Augustinian.

Proust's memory is wholly taken up with the human, it merely resuscitates the past with its finely-wrought detail, its gaps, its successive periods; but, now and then, in the instant of aesthetic perception, it touches a point of eternity, as did Augustine with Monica that evening at Ostia; for instance, in the studio of the painter, Elstir, or listening to Berma, or contemplating with Bergotte on the point of death, that little yellow wall of Vermeer's. But Proust never looks at his life as within God's eternity; the sublimity of his perceptions never touches the depths of the divine.

Likewise that sin of the flesh whose repugnance he conveys to us shuts himself up within himself. He cannot tear himself away from it by the act of remembrance; for though he suffers from it,

even deplores it, he does not look on it as calling
for an act of mercy, whence he could survey it
with some kind of tranquillity. He is compelled
to stay bound to it, and his art itself is impaired
because of it.

GIDE

In *Les Faux-Monnayeurs*, Gide makes this observation: 'The novel is concerned with the vicis-
situdes of life, good fortune and the reverse, social
relations, the war of the passions, with human
characters, but not with the very essence of man'.

It is certainly the case that Gide's earlier novels
are a meditation on the action of the Eternal
Being in time and, in this aspect, may be compared with the experience recounted in the
Confessions.

Our temporal state is an abnormal one; we are
inwardly divided, ever escaping from ourselves
and pouring ourselves out, uncertain, restless and
incapable of *possessing* and even of *being*; this is
admitted. Everyone's desire is to become present
to himself, that is to live in a temporal state in
which the past is no longer finished and ended, the
future no longer uncertain, the present no longer
fluid. The instant wherein all would be compre-
hended would be eternal life.

Many however consider that the eternal present cannot be given in the human form of time, that it must be consigned by hope to a new time which we call eternity and which will be met with after death. This eternity, like the moral life itself, has two poles. Just as there is an absolute distinction between good and evil, so there is a corresponding one between an eternity of life and an eternity of death.

Others hold that the eternal present is to be looked for in time itself. It is a question of preparing certain moments which will have eternal value and solidity; no waiting, then, nor hope. What matters is to find a third dimension of time; whether we call it presence, possession, act, nourishment, it is nothing else than eternity.

That is Gide's position, and his ecstasies of sense call for comparison with St Augustine's ecstasy at Ostia. He may be called the anti-Augustinian *par excellence*.

On the one hand, Gide rejects the absolute distinction of the high and the low, of good and evil. For him man has no *essential quality*, but an *accidental duplicity*, and consequently it is only necessary to throw off the mask of convention and morality to find anew simplicity, nakedness and innocence. But is Gidian man really *simple?*

B

In my opinion, he is not even just a double man but a dissociated one, with so to speak two lives, one supra-sensible of a mystical type, but of an empty mysticism, the other infra-sensible of a sensual type, but of a perverse sensuality. Gidian man possesses a soul (*anima*) and senses (*sensus*), but not what could be called a heart (*cor*).

On the other hand, in opposition to St Augustine, Gide always assumes there is no difference between time and eternity, or at any rate that their difference can always be transcended by realising absolute instants. Let us look into these instants. Are they instants of possession? Not at all; they are instants of indigence, appetency and desire. Of desire that *hopes*? No, but of desire which *aspires*, and whose aspiration will never be realised, so that for Gide the true fashion of having is not to have. Gidian man knows the ecstasy that lifts him up above time; he knows, too, the voluptuousness that abases him below time but he is unaware of that human duration which is time itself and the sacrament of eternity. In these aspects he enables us to understand the Augustinian man whom he rejects.

The ultimate ground of the difference between the two is this.—Like Plotinus, Spinoza, and Gide, St Augustine distinguishes two aspects in human time: one, so to speak, horizontal, which is tension towards the future, *expectatio futurorum*; the other, so to speak, vertical, which is attention to the eternal, *extensio ad superiora*. Spinoza called horizontal time, *duration*; vertical time, *the intellectual love of God*. Gide calls the first, desire; the second, fervour. Both Spinoza and Gide held that, having distinguished these two currents logically, we could separate them *ontologically* by a process of leaving aside all the temporal and keeping only what is, already in this life, the substance of the eternal. Plotinus, Spinoza and Gide thought that this sifting and evading were possible and in their eyes in this lies salvation. Like them St Augustine knew the states of deliverance the soul sometimes experiences through the contemplation of truth; but he saw in them not salvation, but only a foretaste of it. For him, in short, there was but one way of attaining the supreme ecstasy: by separating, once and for all, these two axes of time, so as to leave only the totally pure; and that was by death.[16]

SARTRE

Coming now to Sartre, I will first observe that there is a profound resemblance between him and St Augustine. Sartre's philosophy has always made me think of the Manichaean period of St Augustine.

The essence of Augustine's Manichaeism was his inability to conceive existence except under the form of matter, or, as he said, as *massa*. He held that the spirit itself existed as a kind of 'mass', sprung from matter, a prisoner in its ponderous cage, reduced to a nonentity. This *massa* exists in us, beneath us, as the evil part of ourselves which lives on the *biological* plane, the part to which we are indebted for the two forms of indulgence: the spasm of pleasure and the swelling of pride—the part, in fact, which *sins*. But above the zone taken over by sin there exists a zone in which the spirit is disengaged, un-fettered—that of the being which depends on itself alone, which is always conformed to its ideal, since this ideal and its freedom are inter-mingled.

All this amounts to the affirmation of two theses. One, that the existence of matter, a mass closed in on itself, is primary. The spirit exists at first in a mode analogous to that of matter, shut up in itself and at the same time outside itself—which is concupiscence. Two, that above this existence which is truly *ex*-istent, there is a possibility of absolute freedom unrelated to it. Consequently when, at this time, St Augustine sinned, he did not condemn himself; for it was not his pure freedom which sinned, but there worked in him the evil and 'massive' spirit, the *natura peccatrix* unrelated to himself.

If we turn to the main points of the doctrine set out in *Being and Nothingness*, we will find something analogous. Sartre holds being to be divided into the *In-itself* (En-soi), which is without awareness and material, and the *For-itself* (Pour-soi), which is endowed with awareness and is spiritual. But since the existence of the *In-itself* is prior by right, like the Augustinian *massa*, it follows that, seen from the *In-itself*, the *For-itself* seems a useless excrescence since it adds to the fact of being the absurd extra which is the awareness of being and of suffering. The being which is given to itself becomes suffering, captivity, absurdity, as a spirit imprisoned in matter would be; literally and truly, it is passion and useless passion. Conversely, seen from the *For-itself*, that is conceived, felt, perceived by an awareness, the *In-itself*, that is the thing (an object, this tree before me) is like an unknown entity projected outside its essence, which is therefore *de trop*. Consequently, both from the side of the being-

spirit and from that of the being-body (which,
fundamentally are not so very different, since the
spirit is, as it were, a *massa cogitans*), I find matter
to have the character of an existence which is an
excrescence, a projection and an absurdity.

But though existence is thus indicated and
condemned, it is not so with freedom, provided
this word be taken to mean that which makes the
very ground of our being, that is to say the power
to take up and use for one's own ends what
exists in nature and history, and to give to this
essence, this character, this behaviour which one
chooses, though void of value themselves, the
same sort of love one necessarily has for oneself.
In that case there is a sense in which it matters
little that the existence given to us is 'massive',
material, or to be condemned, or that, since we
are more clear-sighted as regards others than as
regards ourselves, we apprehend with horror this
condemnation of being in the existence of others,
—for in oneself there is pure freedom. It is of
small account to have assigned to existence a
place lower even than that given ordinarily by
philosophers (even the philosophers of *Becoming*),
for freedom is exalted even above the place given
it by moralists (even the moralists of the Ideal
and of Duty); it is, indeed, an extremely high

value to be able to create value. It is, too, an extremely heavy burden to be able to take on oneself the inevitable.

We are here in the presence of a *dualism* carried to extremes; and, no doubt, Sartrism is the strongest expression of that eternal *Catharism* which is the necessary consequence of the denial of a single creative principle. Atheism, in fact, cannot long remain monistic, not long explain the totality of being by a single, identical principle. At least, it can be such only in periods of calm, with persons of optimistic temperament, not subject to interior crises. But, once we experience the rooted evil within us and outside us, we can no longer admit absolute unity. Then it is that, unless we affirm a transcendent principle and a free creature faced with a good it did not make itself, we are obliged to divide being into two parts: one *pura*, the other *impura*, and to assign to our freedom no relation with the impure part.

That is why, in atheistic existentialism, we find of necessity the same type of thought as in the dualistic doctrine of Manes, which St Augustine held for nine years. It is by no means to minimise the doctrine of *Being and Becoming*, set out by Sartre during the last war, to say that St Augustine started from the point at which modern thought seems tempted to end its journey.

*   *   *

We might draw other comparisons besides these; some, in fact, suggest themselves forcibly, as, for example, that of the spirit prompting St Augustine with the general tone of the novels of Mauriac or of Bernanos. These however I omit and pass on to more difficult questions.

A single word could be used to express the difference between St Augustine's inner experience and that of the moderns, however great (with the exception of Claudel):—the word *integrity*. There occurs in one of St Augustine's earliest works a wonderful sentence, extremely compacted and impossible to translate: 'Ego in discernendo et in connectendo unum volo et unum amo. Sed cum discerno purgatum, cum connecto integrum volo.' It may, perhaps, be paraphrased as follows: 'Whether I divide things up or join them together, I have the same end in view, the same object of love. But, when I divide (analyse) them, I aim at their purification; when I rejoin (synthesise) them, it is with a view to their integration.'

St Augustine did indeed aim at achieving, with

the help of the one Mediator, wholeness, the
gathering up of all the powers into a single harmony, the restoration of original integrity impaired by sin. Each degree of being was to be
respected and allotted its due place, but taken up
into a higher order. Here we have Plato redis-
covered, Pascal proclaimed and prefigured. *Integrum volo.*

Ultimately, what we call experience is only too
often a diminution of experience. The sensual
imagine themselves to have experience of the
flesh. St Augustine, with all the memories of his
past, knew that the flesh could be known truly
only from the standpoint of purity recovered. As
Simone Weil said, purity alone has the power to
look on what is sullied. What the analysts and
novelists of to-day call experience is not *integral*
experience, but experience of *disintegration.*

II

SOCIAL MAN IN HISTORY

WE will now leave the side of the mountain that is man in his inner being; and, before settling ourselves on the crest, examine the other slope which is mankind as a whole in time, man in society, the *City of God*. Here, too, what a difference is apparent between St Augustine's ideas and those of the philosophers.

The thinkers of antiquity may be said to have looked on the social order as hierarchical. The distinctions they admitted in society were based on differences of function, those of magistrates, guardians, and workers, as in Plato's Republic, who were free men with acknowledged rights and round whom was gathered a body of slaves on whom the economy depended. The ancient city-state could be likened to a pyramid, a mass independent of time, made up of separate stones each with its special function in the whole structure but all subordinated to the highest of them, for whom all the others exist—the ruler, the man of contemplation.

St Augustine's view was quite different. He likened man's history to a musical work. The idea was suggested by the writers of antiquity, who saw time as a numbered sequence, a rhythm perceived in the revolutions of the stars and their spheres. In any rhythm, we can consider either its repetitiveness which enables us to assign to it a number; or else we can fix our attention on its transitoriness and evanescence. It was this second aspect with which St Augustine was mainly concerned. For him, time was that which it was impossible to take hold of. The nature of the world is to be shifting and transient; and, as we are fixed to a single part of it, we can never be in enjoyment of the whole.

Let us recall how St Augustine analysed the nature of time by scrutinising the simplest of experiences.

Supposing, he says, I am about to sing something I know; before I begin the whole of it is present to my attention. Once I have started, all that part which is over and past rests present in my memory; and so the life of my action is divided into a part in the memory as regards what I have said already, and another part in expectation as regards what I am about to say. Meanwhile, my attention remains in the present and by its means what was to be becomes a thing of the past. According as this movement continues, the area of memory is widened as that of expectation is narrowed, until the moment comes when the latter is itself brought to nothing. Then it is that the action is accomplished and has passed over into the memory.

The analysis can be pushed further and further in each direction, since what applies to the piece as a whole is true, too, of each of its parts, every syllable in fact. The same may be said of a more extensive action of which this act of singing may be but a part; of a whole life, in fact, of which a man's separate actions are so many parts; and also of the history of all the generations of men of which the individual human lives are parts.

We have here a new conception of time or, rather, a different way of being aware of time.

St Augustine did not aim at *holding up* the flow of time at a particular chosen instant. On one occasion he tried to do so and believed himself to have been raised up by grace above the passage of time. But the 'ecstasy at Ostia' left him with a sense of having failed. So then, time never stops and it is no use wanting to halt it; all we can do is to long for its cessation. The best thing for us is to surrender to the passage of time and try to make ourselves harmonise with its course. That is what faith, more than any other activity of the mind, enables us to do, since by it we come to be aware of the gradual working-out of salvation, and this makes of human history a poem.

From this it could easily be anticipated that, as soon as a suitable occasion arose, a new view of history as a whole, based on the similarity between the exterior and interior man, would take shape of its own accord in St Augustine's mind.

Such an occasion was the sack of Rome. On the 24th of August, 410, the Salarian Gate was forced by Alaric's hordes and they encamped below the walls. These barbarians then began the sack of the eternal City, and after six days of pillage withdrew. From far away in Hippo, St Augustine saw the significance of the event. It meant the rupture of the ancient contract binding the soul to earthly cities. It was an illustration of the new alliance between the soul and the true city.

There exists alongside the individual the city of which he is a member and apart from which he would be of no account. But there is an enormous difference between the two. The individual has a destiny of his own; he has scarcely come into existence when he escapes the bonds both of the body and of society. The word 'eternity' has a distinct meaning for him, but it cannot possibly mean anything for the city, which exists solely for temporal convenience and provisionally. There must of necessity arise a conflict between two such opposed ends.

It is a conflict with a long history. It took its rise in the city of antiquity with the pursuit of that unrestricted thought called philosophy. This it was which severed the relation set up of old between the salvation of the soul and exterior worship. Till then the need for salvation, so far from turning man away from the city, had bound him closely to its local gods and rites. At the death of Socrates it would already have been possible to divine that as the idea of salvation became more and more purified, it would shake the ancient cities to their foundations. The master's great disciples, being equally concerned to uphold the political order and to emancipate the spirit, applied themselves to resolving the opposition. Ultimately, even with Plato, this was done to the advantage of the city. The Stoics in their heyday, the heirs of the Aristotelian tradition on this point, looked on the Roman Empire as being the image of a perfect city, universal and impervious to any sort of decay.

St Augustine proceeded to show that the city of the soldiers and politicians was incapable of finding a way to save the State in time. He presented a criticism of the politics and moral teaching of the ancient world, and of popular paganism. Neither the city of the philosophers had discovered a method of saving the soul for eternity, nor the Roman positivists, nor the Platonic philosophy, nor Alexandrine mysticism, nor the African wonderworkers. Porphyry and Apuleius may have spoken about mediation, but it was not a mediation that could bring salvation. The catastrophe of 410 was the sign of a double failure, that of the statesmen and soldiers and their fine social order which could not even make certain of temporal goods, and that of the philosophers and mystics who were unable to assure to men the goods of eternity.

There would have been no choice but to despair, had not the mediation of Christ Incarnate been offered to men. This takes us up into a new order, which is temporal in its course, eternal in its fulfilment. It opens up to man the passage hitherto impossible.

We have a description of this movement. It began with the creation of the angels, for Lucifer's revolt preceded that of Adam; but through the sin of the angel the moral order was split up into two communions, into 'two cities', as St Augustine says, of which one has love for its principle and the other self-love, the counterfeit of love. Evil was brought into the world through the warping of the will. The dichotomy will never come to an end.

Now the human order comes into being. The fall of its first representatives is unfolded before us; we see the beginning of the period in which life is invariably followed by death, the bitter fruit of this fall. The two cities move apart; Cain builds the earthly city, while Abel is a pilgrim on earth. With Moses, however, the city, formerly in pilgrimage, becomes settled; it receives a code of laws, it becomes a people which prepares the coming of the Church. The earthly city has a history of its own, which is that of the Empires, their establishment and their fortunes, particularly of the Roman Empire which comes to replace all the others. The two cities are not always opposed, for the Empire gains from the order coming from religion, and the Church from the establishment of peace. Besides, their real frontiers cannot be distinguished, since the Church has reprobates among its members and some of its children in the ranks of its enemies. This very admixture requires, in justice, a state beyond time wherein the good and the bad will be separated and each go to his own place.

Time will come to an end, and with it the whole political order. The saints, assembled in a perfect society, will reign with Christ. Seen from the vantage-point of the heavenly Jerusalem, in which are found, sublimated, the characteristics of ancient Rome, the horizon stands out clearly; nature is simply a theatre, history but one aspect of the whole context of things, and politics is taken up only with ends of small importance. The earthly Church itself, the sole normal means of salvation, is only a provisional resting-place, an outline structure.

Remember what was said above, in connection with the *Confessions*, about that turning back of the mind on itself, when, after looking at its own life as it was, it seeks to view it in God. It is then that *narratio* is followed by *laudatio*, and they both are conjoined in *confessio*.

The same happens on the collective plane of human history, and it is perfectly natural that St Augustine's mind should pass through the same phases.

So then, after considering human history in itself and according to its *apparent* dimension of pure successiveness, he goes on to view it in God and in the context of predestination from eternity.

From the first, the purely temporal, standpoint Christ was just a Nazarene who made his appearance at a particular time and place, in this *hic et nunc*; and of similar *hics et nuncs* there is an infinite number.

From the new standpoint, however, the whole of history flows in relation to the God-Man. Previously Christ was a golden rivet on the wheel; now he is the nave, itself motionless, on which the wheel revolves.

If it is hard to acknowledge that God enters into history, that is because we fail to grasp the complementary truth that history, through the Incarnation, enters into God.

We must, then, first see the Incarnation as a part of history, and Christ's coming in its temporal setting, that is to say in its place in the annals of political and religious events. Otherwise, the Incarnation would never be anything more than a mythical and insubstantial occurrence. Consequently St Augustine shows with all the learning possible in his day, the place occupied in the whole of history by the Jewish people. He takes care to underline the instances in which the Biblical chronology corresponds with that of other peoples. There were in fact many different civilisations in existence at the same time; along with the history of the Jews, there was the history of Assyria, Greece, Egypt, and Rome. Abraham came on the stage at the time when the Assyrians had their fourth king, the Sicyonians their fifth. The exodus from Egypt took place at the time of Cecrops, Ascatades, Marathus and Triopas. Christ was born in the reign of Herod, when Augustus was emperor. Christianity, then, is not a myth.

But if the Incarnation is no mythical event, it is still not an historical event like any other, one limited to a particular place and time. We have just seen that it is a point in the visible history of the world; we now go on to say that, of the invisible history it is the true centre and focus, for that part of history unfolds within the Incarnation. And it is through the presence of the Word pervading all epochs of time that we are able to transcend time.

No doubt, Christ came *hic et nunc* and his life ceased in the course of time as an arrow is spent at the end of its flight. But yet his teaching is given to men at all times, and his sacrifice (whether known or unknown to men) is at the centre of the moral history of mankind. All good actions are in

relation with his one, perfect offering and all the
sacraments derive from him their efficacy. It
therefore matters little that the Incarnation took
place here and not there, so soon or so late, since
its effects extend to all centuries. It is quite
certain that Christ chose the times of his birth and
death; and this one case enables us to understand
how the dates of things and their allotted place in
the course of time can have a reason known to
God alone. Altogether the Incarnation owes to
chronology no more than a kind of support. In the
spiritual world it is at the centre, and it presides
over the course of history. It is the sole mediation,
the one efficacious theurgy; through it the eternal
comes to the rescue of the temporal and the temporal in turn takes its place in the eternal.

We are now in a position to understand the
relation that obtains between the Jewish past and
the Christian present, between the Church and
the Churches, between the Church and the cities.

Christ is the immutable, eternal word, who
governs every creature both spiritual and cor-
poreal according to its situation in time and place.
This word is always the same, but it is expressed
differently in the different ages of human history.
The mystery of eternal life was proclaimed, from
the very beginning of the human race, by signs

and sacraments appropriate to the time. Then God chose out a people to express in figure his future coming and manifestation of himself, and at the same time he prepared them for it; this was the Jewish people. It had a very special destiny. Its function was to symbolise, to proclaim, to prefigure. Its entire history is explained by its prophetic mission.

Everything, so we read in the *City of God*, not only the prophecies made by word of mouth, not only the moral and devotional precepts contained in the sacred writings, but also the sacred rites, the priests, the tabernacle, the temple, the altars, the sacrifices, the feasts, the ceremonies, and, in general, whatever belongs to the worship of *latria* owing to God—all these are so many figures of what happened in the past, of what is taking place in the present, and of what it is hoped will be fulfilled in the future. And these figures all relate, finally, to eternal life in Christ.

There was no necessity for all the Jews to have grasped the significance of these symbols that they possessed or embodied. A plan was being unfolded and they could be simply its passive instruments. But, if there were those who acted without understanding, there were others who saw the whole significance of what they were doing. These we call, precisely for that reason, prophets. In the midst of a carnal people, they stood out by the light of the interior man. They helped the human race in its turn to rise higher, both by teaching what was demanded by circumstances, and by giving some inkling of what it was premature to explain fully.

So it is that the whole of history is present in each of its parts.

We will take the Paschal feast as an example. In outward appearance and on the level of succession and change, there are two Paschs—the ancient Pasch of the Jews and the new Pasch of the Christian sacrifice, which is emancipated from the Jewish rite and commemorates daily the past event it re-enacts. But in another sense there is only one Pasch, that in which Christ was sacrificed, and this Pasch proclaims the eternal Pasch it inaugurates. Thus the horizontal order of past and future, comprising two Paschs, the Jewish one before Christ which looked to the future, and the Christian one after Christ which turns back to the past, is in some way a figure of a more profound order, a vertical one, comprising both Christ's one sacrifice in time and his eternal sacrifice. The order of past and future intertwines with that of the single and eternal, which absorbs it.

This profound insight of his enabled St Augustine to meet a number of objections raised in his own time, and always recurring, on the relations of Christ and Time, a subject on which M. Oscar Culmann has written an excellent book.

If God desires all men to be saved and wished to found on earth a universal religion, why did he choose such an insignificant race, and why did he wait so long? If Christ is the sole way, what about those who lived so many centuries before him? What has become of all those thousands of souls who cannot be blamed in the slightest degree, since he in whom it is claimed belief is necessary had not yet appeared? In other words, how is it possible to reconcile with God's universal providence the particularism of the Mosaic religion and the lateness of the Incarnation?

The objection would have force if there had ever been a time when the religion of the Incarnation was not available to man. In fact, the Christian religion was present among mankind even before the coming of Christ in the flesh. In those days, however, it was only *universal virtually*, being practised first by a single person, then by a single family, then by a single tribe, and then by a single people.

Must we say that, apart from these privileged

persons, no one at all received the benefit of the gifts of God? This perplexing question St Augustine answered in his letter to Deogratias.

He drew a distinction there between two ways in which God acts for the salvation of men. One is official and collective, the other invisible and individual. Admittedly, he says little about this second way; the controversy with Pelagius made him take up an extreme attitude on the salvation of unbelievers, but he never denied the fact of this way. Granted there was a chosen people, are we to conclude that the elect were confined to this people? St Augustine affirmed that the elect were to be found in all peoples. No doubt, we can never be in a position to judge individual cases, but what we can say is that the salvation this religion offers, just as it was available to all epochs, so it was available, invisibly, to all who were worthy to receive it. So, from the very beginning of the human race, all who believed in the Son of God, or who had any sort of knowledge of him, or who lived according to his laws in holiness and justice, in whatever time or place they lived, were saved through him.

At times, St Augustine was brought to some sort of intimation that the frontiers of the city of the saints do not necessarily coincide with those of the

Church. There belong to the invisible Jerusalem those excommunicated persons who, for the sake of the Church's peace, bear patiently an affront they have not deserved. Within it, as well, should be placed Job the Idumaean, the centurion Cornelius, the Sybil of Cumae who prophesied truly about the last judgment and all who live according to the dictates of conscience. In this way, the gulf separating revelation, which is always particularised, from redemption, which must of necessity be held universal, is mysteriously filled.

'St Augustine', Mgr Batiffol wrote, 'may be said to have glimpsed the doctrine of the soul of the Church' (though he never used the expression), 'the soul to which all those saints belong who have been sanctified by God without belonging to the visible body. The range of action of divine grace does not, in fact, coincide with the area of the *Catholica*, but overflows it on every side to reach the whole of humanity. . . . But this doctrine of the soul of the Church was not one on which he might be tempted to dwell, since, in his battle against the Donatist schism, he was so dependent on the doctrine of the necessity of the visible Church.'

But if the history of the Jews was a prophetic

one and wholly orientated to the future, why does time still go on after Christ has come? And, if it continues, what new thing can it bring, since Christian history is simply the unfolding of what was prefigured of old? After the great coming, how should there be anything else to come?

The doctrine of the Messias explains easily enough the time preceding the day of glory; it is all expectation, preparation, and everything has its significance. But how are we to explain that time continues after the Messias has gone? It is not surprising that the messianic age seemed, to the Jewish prophets and the writers of apocalypses, to coincide with the day of judgment, and that the first Christians could not resist believing in the imminence of the end of the world. What new thing could possibly come into being after that which was newness itself? What is there which could be comparable with the first coming of Christ and his second coming for the judgment? The interval between these two events is, surely, negligible; it could easily be regarded as a single generation, for however immense it might be and whatever should happen in it, nothing essential could take place. Can we not say, with St Paul, that the Christian age is 'the beginning of the end of the world'?

St Augustine partly escapes the danger of thinking in these terms by a theory of sacrifice derived from the teaching of the prophets, a theory which prevented him splitting up history into two parts, as if there were an absolute *before* and *after*.

Like the word *sacramentum*, *sacrificum* takes on, with him, a wealth of meaning which is yet very exact. Sacrifice is any work we perform to unite us to God in a sacred bond, any act done in reference to the sovereign good who alone can make us happy. St Augustine held that the offerings of the Mosaic law were not themselves sacrifices but only figures, professions, *sacramenta*, reminding men of the necessity of the sacrifice of themselves or announcing the coming of the sacrifice of the God-man. Even fraternal charity, under the new law, is sacrifice only if ordered to God and practised out of love for him. A body wholly consecrated to God by temperance, a soul which renews itself by submission to the Unchangeable, every work of mercy done either to one's neighbour or to oneself, contrition and the humiliation of repentance, this is what makes up a true sacrifice; in this way we give back to God not only his gifts but our very being.[16]

But all these sacrifices of men are, ultimately,

related to that of Christ; this is what finishes and perfects them. These offerings together from the City, the universal sacrifice offered to God by the great high priest who in his passion immolated himself for mankind. The sacrifice of Christians therefore consists in their forming together a single body in Christ, and this is the mystery the Church celebrates without ceasing in the sacrament of the altar, in which, by the offering she makes, she offers herself completely.

History does not come to an end with Christ, and the coming of the Messias does not set a bound to time. It is in a sense true that Christ fulfilled the time of preparation. He consigned the Judaism of the letter to a past which was in a way absolute. But the same kind of plan continues, a similar city is in preparation. Only from now on history has another centre. Time is visibly linked up with eternity; and through the mediation of Christ Incarnate the spiritual fruit of the temporal sacrifice is eternal.

Once again, having reached this point, let us pause and see wherein lies the modernity of St Augustine.

Towards the end of the eighteenth century all was ready for the human mind to gain a more exact awareness of time: infinitesimal calculus

which enabled increase to be expressed quanti-
tatively, greater knowledge of historical origins,
budding geology, the political revolutions, the
myth of progress, all these helped the formation
of a philosophy which took human time as its
object, its second nature. Time as it had been
regarded by the philosophers of antiquity was a
'disturbing element', the source of the continual
agitation of things or the constant dissatisfaction
of the soul. It was quite a new thing to see in time
a principle of solidity, growth and consistancy.
The Jews, while they lamented the fact of tran-
science, had the sense of an invisible growth and
increase, as if time was fulfilling creation by carry-
ing it in successive waves towards its triumphant
end, when, as St Paul said, 'God will be all in all'.
But when in the nineteenth century, after dis-
regarding it for so long, philosophy came to concern itself openly with historical time, an ambig-
uity appeared. Its nature will be seen if we compare Hegel with St Augustine.

Hegel

The nineteenth century thinkers possessed,
under different forms, a sense of the meaning of
time which links them together and distinguishes
them from their predecessors in spite of what they

share with them. Hegel is the one we are to consider as being the antitype of St Augustine, since
he worked out both the idea of History and that of
Mediation. M. Brunschvicg was quite right in
saying that 'Hegel's religious experience is,
extended throughout all the speculative and
practical domains, experience of the *Word*, of the
unity which, thanks to reason's role of mediator,
is established between the eternal ground of being
and the reality of nature or of history'.

Hegel saw clearly that to synthesise the individual moments of time and to link its movement with its eternal source there was needed a
being, or a thought, which should subsist simul-
taneously, both in time and in eternity, and so be
capable of uniting the two. It may be, too, that
he saw that this work of mediation could not take
place equally on the two levels that were to be
united, but that it should belong, by its origin, to
the higher of the two and take up to itself the
lower. Something of the sort is suggested by the
philosophy of the Incarnation, since Christ, the
God-Man, is not equally man and God, but God-
made-man. But with Hegel mediation could not
be a real, and, as it were, vertical, one between
an eternal nature and a temporal nature subordinated to the eternal in an indivisible structure. It

is, rather, a logical and horizontal mediation, which follows the course of history and where each term, once attained, becomes in turn a means to go beyond itself. We might say that with Hegel, the moment a Mediator is dispensed with, there is no longer any mediation, but only middle terms posited in Becoming, or rather, which are themselves Becoming. In fact they hardly seem to deserve to be called either *middle* or *terms*, since they are means without leading to an end, terms which are necessarily transcended.

With Marx we can catch sight of an attempt to take away from Hegel's 'mediation' its property of being only logical and not real. Marx, it would seem, aimed at introducing into the very root of the interconnection of historical periods a mediation that was perceptible and concrete, working, too, and suffering, one co-extensive with the whole of humanity, ever growing in self-consciousness, and the equivalent of what, in Christianity, St Paul calls *unus mediator homo Christus Jesus*. Just as the Christian enjoys by his participation in Christ an advance possession of the kingdom, and as he contemplates in Christ the End become Means, the Truth become Way, so, too, the Marxist has that which corresponds in his sphere; for between the objective historical situation of the present moment and the revolution to come there exists a concrete mediation which is that of the organised proletariat. This myth is that which corresponds to the 'nature' of the carpenter of Nazareth which is possessed by the Form of God, the proletariat being as it were the matter, the political organisation the form.

Humanity then will be reconstructed with the *Proles-rex* as its centre, as in Christianity it is centred on Christ. In this proletariat become a single community, as in the Christ-Church, the soul of each individual, incarnated in his work as if in a second body, is already in possession of the essence of the *Eternal being of the future* whose coming he helps to prepare. The comparison might be pushed further still; and, in each case, there would be seen a separation of the 'good' from the 'wicked', the *treacherous* presence of the wicked among the good, the *concealed* presence of the good among the wicked. They are the same archetypes in both. All this goes to show in Marx (as, no doubt unconsciously, in Spinoza and Jewish thought after Christ) an attempt to find an equivalent of the Incarnation, but without God or Christ; without personal immortality, but strongly endowed with the power of actualising itself. Furthermore, with Marx more than with anyone else, this attempt stoops down to the most indigent and insignificant part of the human race. Marx *annihilates* Hegel's logical myth; he gives it the form of a slave, making it palpable, bleeding, crucified—in expectation of a marvellous future.

Yet the more he approximates to Christianity, the more remote he becomes. Even with Marx, it is ultimately no more than a question of a logical mediation, excogitated by the philosopher in his study, enforced by the politician or the soldier, but without any of the reality of the man Jesus, who really lived and suffered. The only reality attaching to this proletariat which finally comes to organise human history is that of a reality in becoming, ever destroying and recreating itself without end since time is a kind of indefinite spiral. Besides, since the persons who serve as instruments of this mediation have no eternity of their own to look for, and universal history is without consciousness of its own process, there is no possible foundation for its continuance in the same course.

That is, no doubt, how a follower of St Augustine would answer Hegel or Marx. He and they would understand one another, through what they had in common: a sense of totality, of mankind seen in all its dimensions, a sense of becoming, a

c

sense of the dramatic and logical nature of history, a sense of action, hardship, suffering, a sense of ever-present mediation. But for a logical and indefinite mediation the Augustinian would sub-stitute the concrete, single mediation of an Eternal being within history, who alone could bring about the sublimation and divinisation of all men, taking each individually.

It may be that the reason why Hegelianism was unable to safeguard the singularity of being lies in the absence, with these philosophers of change, of any interior experience of historical succession. I have pointed out that, to St Augustine, the his-tories of mankind, of a period, of a life, of a day, an hour, a song, a syllable, a single vowel . . . are all analogous, and perhaps, ultimately, identical. In every case the moments perceived by analysis form a continuous series; they complete one an-other and are interconnected; in the Augustinian saying so beloved of Claudel, the universe is the *melody of a sublime artist* and the parts of the song pass quickly, speeding along at the behest of the artist, himself motionless, who sees them forming a single unity like objects joined together in one space. Thus to someone who could see the whole course of history in a single view, time would contract to a vibration. (It was in this sense that

Bergson, in seeking to understand the relation of eternity to time in motion, used to point to the millions of successive vibrations that the eye contracts into a single, motionless colour.) As for us, we are limited by being within time, and we can only grasp all times at once by making use of imagination. Faith alone, by the idea it gives of universal history, enables us to understand the passage of time, and to see that it is negligible in comparison with eternity.

Moreover, this time of history and the eternal being are not brought into communication by an act of the intelligence, as Hegel thought—by *ratio* alone, as we would say—but by a more complex act which, indeed, has *ratio* for its basis, its matter, but gives it a special structure by adding to it another dimension (as the third dimension of space makes the circle into a sphere). This act is prayer, *oratio*.

Ratio, if we follow it exclusively, leads to purely linear and temporal dialetic, as is the case with the modern dialecticians. *Ratio* believes itself to have grasped and possessed the curve traced by time, but fails to perceive the immovable and higher source of this curve. It is like the thought of some being placed at the point of a compass describing a circle and unable either to see or understand that there is a hand, in another dimension, guiding its course. It is by *oratio*, at every instant of life, that *ratio* is completed. It reaches out darkly to the future for which it prays; it seeks to blot out all in the past that is not eternal. It submits to the plan it cannot see and adheres to it by faith. St Augustine has left to us in outline a metaphysics of prayer.

III

THE UNION OF INTERNAL AND EXTERNAL HISTORY

Now that we have examined the two facts of St Augustine's thought, that concerned with the interior man and that dealing with mankind as a whole, both in the historical aspect, there is one observation to be made.

What is characteristic of St Augustine is not that he investigated either one of these subjects, nor that he investigated both of them, but that he divined that they were related to one another. We will now try to take up our position on the high ground that unites the two slopes. It is by no means easy, for it is hard to see things together in one view. As Pascal says, all is one, and one thing is in another.

What we can at least do from this elevated position is to gain an idea of where lie the shortcomings of our own age. There are some who are preoccupied solely with the interior man; these are the novelists, the spiritual writers, the existentialists of today. Others consider only the exterior man; they are the sociologists, the statisticians and cyberneticians, the dialecticians. Truly, there are many modern writers with a genius for introspection who have explored the spiritual sphere, as, for instance, Maine de Biran and Bergson. But life is short and it is now almost impossible to devote oneself to history without excluding all other pursuits. Bergson, towards the end of his life, had a great desire to study the history of God's dealings with man.

There have been writers in modern times who studied and worked out the process of man's historical development. Hegel and Comte applied themselves to understanding mankind as a whole; but their experience and dialectic were imperfect, being unsupported by experience of a spiritual nature. What strikes us in the lives of each is its interior spiritual void. Auguste Comte, and particularly Renouvier and Cournot, who might have achieved this difficult harmony, lacked an experience of the spiritual on a level with their wealth of knowledge. Perhaps we ought to admit that in the present time when knowledge takes up all our energies, when we are no longer content with approximations, this harmony is unattainable by a single person; that it can only be realised in a community, where each member has his distinct sphere of activity. But where is there to be found a community living and united by a rooted faith outside the Church? St Augustine was able to achieve this harmony, because in his day history was still in its first stages.

Among the thinkers belonging to the Catholic family, I know only one whose experiences of the spiritual and the historical order illuminated and strengthened one another, and so deserves the name given to him by Father Przywara of *Augustinus redivivus*, Augustine come back to earth. That man is Newman.

NEWMAN

It is enough to point to the two pairs of books, the *Confessions* and the *City of God* on the one hand, the *Apologia* and the *Development of Christian Doctrine* on the other. They might be given the titles, *De duratione interna* and *De duratione universi*. We could say that the treatises *De Gratia* and *De Ecclesia* were written by St Augustine and Newman in turn, in an inimitably personal way.

Newman experienced conversion, but in a different way to St Augustine. He was preserved from all that suffering that the resistance of the flesh adds to the other trials of conversion, whereas St Augustine never enjoyed the deep calm which goes with the gradual passing from partial to perfect light, which gave Newman such an acute sense of the Church's own development. In other words, Newman had not to accomplish a complete revolution, a 'metastrophe' in the Platonic sense. If he travelled *ex umbris et imaginibus ad veritatem*, he did so not by an uprooting of the will, but through his mind working on the data of history. St Augustine had the greater agony to go through, he was more akin to the rest of men in his experience of the flesh. Newman's experience, being wholly intellectual, can be understood only by the few who have studied the history of the Church or whose wonder has been aroused by the changes of religion.

For this reason, Newman *the just* is surpassed by Augustine the *sinner* in the matter of interior experience. What Newman owed to Augustine was the example of dialogue in solitude of the Creator with the creature, and the idea of thinking and acting as if there were none but *God and me* in the world. Newman did not build up a system on this idea (like Descartes and Leibniz), nor a mystical doctrine (like St Teresa of Avila), but it led him by way of *soliloquy* to *autobiography*. The continuous conversation of the solitary soul with God took place, with both Newman and Augustine, not in a wilderness with occasional ecstasies, but by reflection on life, its contingencies, temptations, projects, failures, sins. Consequently, with both, the intellectual approach took on quite a new form thanks to the contribution brought by prophetic or apostolic experience, which gave considerable scope to historical contingency, to the divine 'happening'.

A fourth century thinker, brought up on Platonism or Aristotelianism, might have been tempted to underrate the historical side of Christianity through looking on world history as just a logical dream.

Still more is the twentieth century thinker brought up on positivism or post-kantian idealism, liable to underrate Christian history through seeing it as a mere dialectical becoming, without any real drama.

So we have Plato on the one side with Hegel on the other over against Christ and his first interpreters, less intent, however, on destroying his message than in emptying it of meaning through taking away that part which concerns existence in time.

From this point of view, Augustine's work is like Newman's in that their experience of a creative force at work within things, an experience derived from what happened to them personally, led them both to reflect on history and to discover there the presence of this same inner force—the Catholic Church discharging in the history of mankind the role that self-consciousness plays in the life of the individual.*

They were, too, both opposed to a philosophy that joined together the temporal and eternal in a single Empire. The imperial organisation gathering all men into one city, and the logical or dialectical organism uniting all concepts and all moments round a single focal point are both of them means, one political, the other philosophical,

---

* In both cases the experiences and doctrines extended beyond the sphere in which they were first applied. Newman, as Przywara saw, introduced elements which, applied to the philosophies of Hegel and Kierkegaard, could provide them with a quite original solution. Like Kierkegaard, he had experienced interior Christian time, not in the form of the *separating instant* capable of possessing the Infinite, but in the form of a *duration capable of receiving the Eternal according to its mode*; and in this he renews contact with an Augustinian tradition that the Reformers had either not known or broken with. More especially, he provided an answer to Hegel (like a Plato who had read Aristotle) by showing that the real becoming of history (which he did not deny, which had, in fact, occasioned his conversion to the Church of Rome, so remote from Anglican immobility) was not a God-making-himself, an immanent dialectic, but that this becoming, *on a certain privileged axis*, was directed by a divine Idea; that History, at least on this axis, had a meaning.

of eliminating the difference between eternity and time by endowing temporal activity with the necessary and beatifying character which belongs to eternity. That is why, as may be seen in Stoicism, Hegelianism and Marxism, the philosophies of the eternal-temporal form a justification of the Empires of their time.

Over against these philosophies and these polities stands the Jewish and Christian tradition. At a time when Christianity was barely implanted, when Greek and Roman thought might have set up an imperial pantheism, St Augustine laid the metaphysical, psychical, political foundations of a Christian view of the world; and it was his work that influenced the period of transition.

Newman foresaw the spread of general disbelief, dominant over the minds of men who would be assailed by the principles of atheism before they had time to discover Christianity. A new deluge, he said, will cover the world and only a very few heights will be left untouched, for men 'will believe in atheism before discovering revelation'. Then a new evangelisation will be needed, but it will be more difficult than the first, since what it has to proclaim will not be a New Thing. The majority will think that Christianity has been finally refuted. As to those who persist in believing, no one will condescend to listen to them or to enter on a discussion. Whatever reply be made, it will amount to saying: it has been refuted once, it is not for us to refute it over again. Newman's work may be said to consist in adapting the Church in advance to this work. It may be that, after a new deluge, the future will see a gradual reconquest of the regions of the spirit, one by one. It will be harder than the original conquest was, for ignorance, however primitive, is a less formidable obstacle than a learned and self-satisfied negation.

IV

ST AUGUSTINE'S PLACE IN THE HISTORY OF EUROPE

WE can now approach with rather more confidence the tremendous question stated at the beginning of this essay, the mystery of predestination. St Augustine, following St Paul, viewed it from the standpoint of mankind as a whole, for it would be unduly rash to try to see its application in a particular case.

After the fall of Rome it was possible to envisage the approaching end of a world. All that had value, the unity of the human race, culture, the security in order which the Romans called peace, tradition, the assurance even the Church drew from the support of the civil power, all this was on the decline. Was this decline to continue indefinitely? The history of the spiritual element in mankind shows, as in a vibrating string, points of expansion and contraction. In one privileged sector a purer element of humanity advances, develops, and seems likely to fecundate the whole earth; but corruption supervenes, accompanied by what seem disasters and the triumph of grosser elements, and the 'chosen people' is broken up and dispersed. Everything leads to the belief that the spirit is on the point of departure; but what looks like the end becomes a new beginning and history starts off again to sow a new seed. The Jewish prophets were strongly conscious of this rhythm in the affairs of men as shown in Abraham's descendants. It was symbolised in the story of the Ark. Isaias spoke of the small *remnant* that continued to be; and the whole ground of the Jewish hope lay in the affirmation that a *remnant* would persist, that the earth would always *bud forth* a saviour.

We may say that in the fifth century of the Christian era in the West one of these difficult transition periods had come. But we might have expected that the *remnant* (as regards thought) would be a School of theologians, perhaps some *diaspora* of prophets widely separated in place but acting to a common end, as were the Fathers of the Church in the East, who wrote in Greek and upheld the Byzantine culture. These 'Greek Fathers' were hardly known in the West. The Western Church was comprised in the Latin culture and that in turn was summed up in St Augustine.

Periods of decline favour the appearance of

genius, that chance product, so improbable yet substantial and enduring. It is, said Hegel, 'at the decline of day that Minerva's bird takes flight'. When the old syntheses break up, their bonds loosened, their matter scattered, the elements now free but unable to remain in a state of anarchy, seek some principle of fresh unity; and this principle or germ is in itself a unity. Then the course of events which seeks to continue, centres on a man apart, whether an originator or a reformer, who takes up what of the past is still living to make it the foundation of the future. But the work of founders and reformers subsists mainly by its consequences, and their names are easily forgotten. The only ones who are really *reborn* are those whose command of language makes their writings last, such as Plato, Virgil, Dante, Shakespeare. Men like these could well console us for the disappearance of a civilisation, if their writings remained, for they are each of them a world, and anyone who had assimilated their work alone would have a world of thought at his disposition. M. de Saci once said to Pascal that he could find in St Augustine alone all the original utterances of Pascal himself.

We may recall St Augustine's analysis of time. A song, which passes in time, is never given in itself, since the sounds which make it up are constantly flowing. But the memory, he says, preserves it and gives it stability. Likewise, in the fifth century when everything rushed headlong, vanished and seemed to be lost for ever, there appeared the art and thought of St Augustine, which gave this flight a fixed and stable form.

There are several types of posthumous existence. Some cease altogether, for they derive merely from the fashion of a time. Others are retained because they are bound up with a political or religious tradition; others, as in Stendhal's case, turn out to be contemporary with a succeeding age. With St Augustine, it is quite otherwise; he is not born anew as a result of chance, but he forms a part of the essence of a human group with its descendants, of a civilisation which recovers self-consciousness in him. This continued life of his has no parallel except in that of Plato whom he resembles and whose thought he hands on.

In Plato there were present in the fullest degree the conditions necessary for survival, though he was not preceded, sustained and continued by a Church. But he founded a School, perhaps the first to have done so, one which resembled a monastic order, provided with rules governing the succession. His works, too, were often obscure

enough to be deemed sacred and to demand inter-
pretation. They have their light and their more
weighty passages, but always pulsate with life;
and, through the dialogue form, so lifelike, they
seem to create themselves anew with every fresh
reading. In them are found intermingled elements
from so many different sources, so many kinds of
inspiration, that any reader, no matter what his
taste, may find food for the mind. Above all they
contain all that was most solid in the preceding
tradition. The errors which ever recur are there
rejected, but they are depicted as possessing a
dignity and, sometimes, an elegance of their own.
Heraclitus, Parmenides, Gorgias, and even Calli-
cles are by no means diminished by their presenta-
tion in the Dialogues; and if they are made use of
to be refuted, it is with far less severity than St
Augustine uses against his opponents, Faustus,
Pelagius or Julian of Eclanus. Plato sets forth
myths derived from common recollection and
easy to retain, the equivalent of a Genesis and an
Apocalypse, bordering uncertainly on ecstasy and
mystery. He gives us a philosophy of politics, of
education, of poetry, and a mystique of love. We
find in his work politicians, women, young men in
great number, gods, and there is always present
the almost too real personality of Socrates who

had the advantage of being able to bring the pure Idea down to earth.

St Augustine, though lacking Plato's suppleness and versatility of talent, and devoid of humour, had the same sort of advantages. Christ was, so to speak, his Socrates, though on an incomparably higher level; for Christ, being divine, was not an object of contemplation but the very source of it.

It is true that St Augustine, who had never heard Christ, could not present him in vivid fashion. But his own personal history, with all the various episodes in his journey towards God, the continual reverberance of it in his memory, the repentance ever accompanying the memory—all this gives his writing a quality of personal witness, the lack of which makes any work even though otherwise excellent seem defective to us, familiar as we are with the Gospel. But what Plato borrowed from the story of Socrates and the hemlock, St Augustine possessed on his own account; he lived it in virtue of his conversion constantly renewed.

St Augustine felt no need to found a School. He had the equivalent of a School in the Church, to which he committed his thought to unite to its own. At the most, what he did was to give a rule of life to a few disciples. As he grew older, he gave up the idea of a monastery of thought and discussion which had attracted him so much at the beginning of his conversion. It must be remembered, also, that round about 420 any foundation of a School was out of the question. As with us in 1940, it was a time of chaos—in other respects, a time very favourable to a work of creation, for a written work can be constructed in the very abyss, when it is helped on by the dissolution of the elements of the world, and when surrounded by an atmosphere of indifference like the mist upon which Virgil looked as the garment of the gods.

Both Plato and Augustine had, as well as preeminent genius, an accidental greatness, owing to the catastrophes of the age. A man is always nobler and greater when he is alone,* and still more so if those who should have accompanied him have disappeared.

The centuries which followed Plato, and those following Augustine, saw a period of emptiness in which it might well have been asked if culture

* It is true that Plato's complement and balance followed him at once, in the person of Aristotle, while St Augustine's Aristotle (St Thomas) did not appear for a long time. Plato was less solitary than St Augustine; for he and Aristotle were twin summits of one mountain, the comparison of one with the other was richly rewarding, and that contributed to the fame of each.

were going to vanish altogether, and then an attempt by the survivors to rebuild the tradition. By then this could be done only by a *Letter*, for, continuity being broken, memory was insufficient. So it was that the Platonic *Scripture* came to be held in especial veneration.

In this connection it may be noticed that what makes a work of original thought survive is its style. That alone lasts long which pleases, as Pascal must have felt when he examined what made up the art of pleasing. All Scripture is like the wreckage of a ship after a storm, and a wreckage has beauty on account of its gaps, its strange shapes, the treasures vaguely anticipated, and all the gifts left by the dead.

At this point we may ask if the recapitulation of tradition round *a single* survivor does not mean an alteration of it, since it is then depicted in the exclusive colours of an individual mind and career. The qualities, then, of an individual destiny are liable to be taken by many generations as rules of thinking, as governing man's aims and feelings.

We may wonder if it is not the case that the very defects of Plato, the rarefied geometrician, the so abstract lover, the remorseless political planner, have been canonised as part of Platonism; if, after twenty-five centuries, we are not still suffering from having inherited Plato's temperament along with his teaching, in spite of Aristotle's mitigations. (Some day the question may be asked about Pascal.)

Likewise, we may wonder to what degree Christianity still suffers from St Augustine's pessimism, which is explicable by his temperament, the circumstances of his passionate and brooding youth, and his nine years' association with the Manichaeans. Why should a people necessarily bear permanently the image of what, for better or worse, a single individual once underwent?

Still, we have to remember that this is a condition belonging to any human work. Any work must have an originator, and be rooted in the circumstances in which it rose. No doubt, as it grows, it seeks to rid itself of its first colouring but it cannot always do so. Nor can it ever do so completely.

Christ's work itself knew these limitations, the price to be paid for any effective presence of the Spirit within history, for any incarnation.

The spirit of Christianity could have been expressed in the most diverse languages; it could have coalesced with a number of different mentalities. It is, however, a matter of history that it was developed and handed on to the Western mind by Judaeo-Greeks. This initial contingency continues to have effect. It is a fact that the first apologists attempted to join the new preaching with the ancient culture and that their work was made easier by the writings of Plato and his disciples of Alexandria. It is a fact that St Augustine rid himself of his obsession with pantheism and dualism by reading Plotinus, and that a mind so steeped in the Gospel first came to a knowledge of itself through the *Enneads*. It is a fact that St Augustine, when a slave to the flesh, was freed only by a favour which he regarded as wholly gratuitous and that he based on this his doctrine of grace. Lastly, it is a fact that, with the separation of the East and the eclipse of Greek culture, Latin theology, derived from St Augustine, dominated the Middle Ages, and inspired the Reformers. So from St Thomas to Malebranche, from St Bernard to Jansenius, the history of theology and philosophy was bound up with the fortunes of Augustinism, just as if this were a second tradition mingled with the first, as if it had given, on the threshold of the new age, a new version of the Christian message.

This being so, no wonder there is a temptation

to equate the Christian *spirit* with the Augustinian *mentality*. My own view is that, from the fifth century onwards, the Church has been attempting, by degrees, to keep in St Augustine's teaching what in him belonged to her spirit and to drop what derived solely from his own cast of mind.

But when all is said and done it must be admitted that we owe to him far more light than shade. Suppose he had never been in the Western and Latin part of the Church. What would have happened?

No doubt we would still have had the essence of the Christian religion, a revelation expressed in dogmatic formularies and in Scripture. *Doctrines* and *duties*, that is the simple, positive religion of the Latins, of St Cyprian for example. But, left to these practical people, we should never have had a 'Christian philosophy', by which I mean a union of faith and intelligence, apart from mystical elevations of the mind or purely moral reflections. We may question whether a Christian philosophy is desirable, or even possible. At one time, too, it was questioned whether 'philosophy' was possible; Socrates showed that movement was possible by walking. Likewise St Augustine showed the reality of a philosopher who was always Christian or of a Christian who was, nevertheless, a philosopher;

and the paradox seems as if it will last as long as
the civilisation of the West. We may even say that
all that is new in Western philosophy since his
time, even the anti-Christian philosophies, so
numerous from the sixteenth century onwards,
was fostered in Augustinian soil by methods
borrowed from him and that they are all trans-
positions or inversions of Augustinism, like those
of Spinoza, Kierkegaard or Hegel, not to mention
others more recent.

That being so, it may well be asked what would
have happened to the West if there had been
nothing corresponding to Augustinism to adapt it
in advance to the struggles and contributions to
come, so as to prevent it being shattered by the
struggles or submerged by the new arrivals. Thus,
as regards the contribution of Aristotle, which St
Thomas turned to such advantage, how could it
have been taken up without ill effect, had there
not been already present a germ of Augustinism
to guard scholasticism against the pressure of that
pre-hegelianism which was the system of Aristotle?

The danger was all the greater in that, as G.
de Plinval observed, in many points St Augustine
is more modern than St Thomas. Though living
in a non-scientific age, he had a scientific mind.

He was remarkably ignorant of mathematics, as he was of Greek and Hebrew; but ignorance is no misfortune, if it enables one to avoid false certainty and leaves intact the power of intuition. The *De Musica* and the *De Ordine* treat in quite modern fashion of number, relativity, and discontinuity; and it may be noted that St Augustine, more of a Platonist than Plato himself, never admitted astrology, nor the eternal cycle of things, nor messages from the dead to the living. If we read the myths of Plato and Plotinus, we are struck with Augustine's sobriety in the matter of images concerning the condition of the spirits in heaven or hell; likewise, if we read St Gregory's *Moralia*, with its stories of persons who have come back to life, we can appreciate his caution.

This is, no doubt, all to be ascribed to his philosophical turn of mind, or else to the purity of his idea of God, and perhaps also to an unconscious independence of his own period. 'Three centuries of profound changes and revolutions in every sphere of life, together with the myriad events and ideas they have seen, perforce make it seem to posterity absurdly naïve and odd, and at times quite incomprehensible, that we are essentially the outcome of what took place in times so different from ours.' What Valéry said on the subject of Bossuet ought to apply still more strongly here, but, in fact, to St Augustine it does not apply at all.

From the standpoint of faith we would be naturally inclined to say that God, in raising up persons of singular endowments, founders or rather recapitulators, always applies 'his law of economy'. What he did with Plato for philosophy and was to do with St Benedict for the monastic life, with St Teresa of Avila for mystical experience, he did, correspondingly, for Christian thought in the West with St Augustine. It is indeed curious to see how those very general disciplines we call *philosophy*, *monastic life*, *mystical life* are stamped by the mentality and even the idiosyncrasies of the person who gave them impetus. Wherever there are people who think in a Christian way, they bear some resemblance with St Augustine, that 'Father' of the Church. It is not merely that they continue or comment on one or other of his ideas, but, for better or worse, something much more far-reaching. They bear within their own being some hormone derived from that so individual destiny and from such extraordinary circumstances. St Augustine's own history, his carnal and zoroastrian phase, his controversy with the monk of Brittany have, in this way, become part and parcel of our intellectual climate.

———————

Now, once again, it seems as if the historical universe is to undergo a radical change. As in the fifth century of our era, civilisation is both concentrated and divided. It seems to be getting ready to be transformed in a fashion impossible to foresee. We belong to an age in which the old structures are collapsing, when the worst seems possible (even the end of our race) when, none the less, there are many signs which give hope of a new synthesis round a rejuvenated Catholic centre.

Here it is that we can profit from the example of the solitary bishop of Hippo. St Augustine lived at a time when it was not easy to hope in a future for humanity. He prepared for death while dictating the last pages of the *City of God* in his episcopal see, which was being besieged by 'barbarians' and defended by Arians—an image of the isolation of those who, while they seek absolute and pure truth, have to compound with the necessarily impure forces of the temporal power. St Augustine could well think himself one of the last generation of men and a witness of the end of time. But the idea of the end of the world is a deceptive one; the things of time die to be born again. And, when fate has placed one in a period when the established order seems about to break up, since the face of the future is impossible to discern, it is best to turn the mind towards the *eternum internum*. In that way, without being aware of it, as did St Augustine, we prepare the manifold future.

NOTES

1 'When I was deliberating about whether I would now start to serve God, as I had long desired, it was *I* who willed, and *I* who willed not; I, I it was. I did not wholly wish, nor was I wholly unwilling. So I contended with myself, and I was divided by myself', *Conf.*, VIII, 22.

2 'And you stirred me up by internal goads, making me impatient until I could obtain certainty by interior vision', *Conf.*, VII, 12.

3 'For thy hands, O my God, in thy hidden providence did not abandon my soul, and sacrifice was offered for me from the blood of my mother's heart through the tears she shed day and night, and thou dealt wonderfully with me', *Conf.* V, 13.

4 'So then how wretched I was, and how thou acted on me to make me feel my wretchedness', *Conf.* VI, 9.

5 'And behold thou art at hand, setting us free from our miserable errors, and establishing us in thy way, consoling us with the words, "Run on, I will bear you and lead you, and bring you there",' *Conf.* VI, 26.

6 'For the steps of man are guided by the Lord, and he wills the Lord's way. Else how could there be salvation, unless thy hand remade what thou made?' *Conf.* V, 13.

7 'And yet I sinned, O Lord my God, orderer and

creator of all things in nature, but of sins orderer only', *Conf.* I, 16.

8 *De dono persev.*, 21-23.

9 'Thou mayst not abandon him who now calls on thee, for, before I called on thee, thou went before urging me repeatedly to hear thee from afar, to be converted and to call on thee who wast calling me.' *Conf.* XIII, 1.

10 'And I erred in my pride, and I was carried about by every wind, and, in deep secrecy, I was being governed by thee', *Conf.* IV, 23.

11 'Therefore thou didst work with me so that I was persuaded', V, 14.

12 'But thou, in thy profound designs granting the essence of what she wished (Monica), didst not heed what she then sought, in order to do in me what she always sought', *Conf.* V, 15; cf. *In Job*, CII, 13.

13 'But thou, most high and most near, most hidden and most present', VI, 4. 'Thy mercy ever faithful from afar continued to encompass me', III, 5. 'But thou, more inward to me than my inmost being and higher than my highest', III, 11. 'Thou alone art present even to those who have become far from thee', V, 2. 'O that they might see the eternity within', IX, 10.

14 'For thou art supreme and unchanging, nor does today run its course in thee, and yet it does flow in thee because all things are in thee; for they would have no course to run if thou didst not contain them', I, 10. 'And thou remainest in thyself, but we are turned about in what we experience', IV, 10.

15 'And therefore he is the source, because, unless he remained while we wandered from the way, there would be no place for us to return to', XI, 10.

16 'What all men call sacrifice is the sign of the true sacrifice', *De Civ. Dei*, X, 5. 'So then true sacrifice is every work of ours done in order that we may be joined in a holy union with God, every work, that is, directed to that final good, which can make us truly blessed. . . . Hence man himself consecrated to the name of God and vowed to him, inasmuch as he dies to the world to live to God, is a sacrifice', *Ibid.*, X, 6.